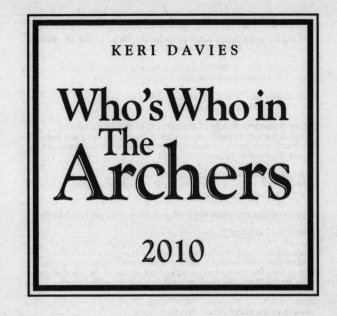

KERI DAVIES

Who's Who in The Archers

2010

BBC BOOKS

1 3 5 7 9 10 8 6 4 2

This book is published to accompany the BBC Radio 4 serial *The Archers*.
The editor of *The Archers* is Vanessa Whitburn.

Published in 2009 by BBC Books, an imprint of Ebury Publishing.
A Random House Group Company.

Main text by Keri Davies. Additional text by Chris Arnot.
Copyright (c) Woodlands Books 2009

The Random House Group Limited Reg. No. 954009.
Addresses for companies within the Random House Group can be found
at www.randomhouse.co.uk

A CIP catalogue record for this book is available from the British Library.

ISBN 978 1 846 07789 0

The Random House Group Limited supports The Forest Stewardship
Council (FSC), the leading international forest certification organisation.
All our titles that are printed on Greenpeace approved FSC certified paper
carry the FSC logo. Our paper procurement policy can be found at
www.rbooks.co.uk/environment

Commissioning editor: Albert DePetrillo
Project editors: Steve Tribe and Kari Speers
Typeset in Garamond Light
Printed and bound in Great Britain by CPI Cox & Wyman, Reading, RG1 8EX.

Events in Ambridge are constantly changing, but we have done our best to
make *Who's Who in The Archers 2010* accurate at the time of publication.

Official Archers Website: bbc.co.uk/archers, to listen again to *Archers*
episodes, including podcasts and an audio archive of the last seven days.
The site also features daily plot synopses, news, information, a map of
Ambridge, a detailed timeline, archive moments, quizzes and chat.

Official Fan Club: Archers Addicts www.archers-addicts.com

Having spent the early part of his life flitting between jobs as varied
as writing advertising copy to serving in the RAF, Keri Davies found
lasting happiness in Ambridge in 1991. A former senior producer for
the programme, he is currently an Archers scriptwriter and runs the
programme's official website.

Chris Arnot, who has been a freelance journalist for 18 years and an
Archers listener for much longer, writes for the *Guardian* and has been a
contributor to the *Independent*, the *Daily Telegraph* and *The Observer* as
well as Radio 4's long-forgotten *Afternoon Shift*.

WELCOME TO AMBRIDGE

We're delighted that our handy guide to the characters and locations in The Archers has reached its eleventh edition.

The book takes into account another exciting year in Ambridge, including Matt's impending trial, Tom and Brian's bust-up over bangers, Mike and Vicky's wedding, and a crisis at The Bull for Sid, Jolene and Fallon.

We hope you enjoy getting up to date – and we hope you like the new look.

Vanessa Whitburn
Editor, *The Archers*

FREQUENTLY ASKED QUESTIONS

When and how can I hear the programme?
On BBC Radio 4 (92–95 FM, 198 LW and on digital radio and television). Transmission times: 7pm Sunday to Friday, repeated at 2pm the next day, excluding Saturdays. An omnibus edition of the whole week's episodes is broadcast every Sunday at 10am. It can also be heard world-wide via podcasts or the BBC iPlayer (go to the *Archers* website: bbc.co.uk/archers).

How many people listen?
Nearly five million every week in the UK alone. *The Archers* is the most popular non-news programme on BBC Radio 4, and the most-listened-to BBC programme online.

How long has it been going?
Five pilot episodes were broadcast on the BBC Midlands Home Service in Whit Week 1950, but *The Archers*' first national broadcast was on 1 January 1951. Episode 15,908 went out on 1 October, 2009, making this comfortably the world's longest-running drama series.

How did it start?

The creator of *The Archers*, Godfrey Baseley, devised the programme as a means of educating farmers in modern production methods when Britain was still subject to food rationing.

So it's an educational programme?

Not any more. *The Archers* lost its original educational remit in the early 1970s – but it still prides itself on the quality of its research and its reflection of real rural life.

How is it planned and written?

The Editor, Vanessa Whitburn, leads a ten-strong production team and nine writers as they plot the complicated lives of the families in Ambridge, looking ahead months or sometimes years in biannual long-term meetings. The detailed planning is done at monthly script meetings about two months ahead of transmission. Each writer produces a week's worth of scripts in a remarkable 13 days.

... and recorded?

Actors receive their scripts a few days before recording, which takes place every four weeks in a state-of-the-art studio at the BBC's premises in the Mailbox complex in central Birmingham. Twenty-four episodes are recorded digitally in six intensive days, using only two hours of studio time per thirteen-minute episode. This schedule means that being an *Archers* actor is by no means a full-time job, even for major characters, so many also have careers in film, theatre, television or other radio drama.

What's that 'dum-di-dum' tune?

The Archers' signature tune is a 'maypole dance': 'Barwick Green', from the suite *My Native Heath* by Yorkshire composer Arthur Wood.

How did you get that news item in?

Episodes are transmitted three to six weeks after recording. But listeners are occasionally intrigued to hear topical events reflected in that evening's broadcast, a feat achieved through a flurry of rewriting, re-recording and editing on the day of transmission.

CHARACTERS BY FORENAME

The characters in this book are listed alphabetically by surname or nickname. If you only know the forename, this should help you locate the relevant entry.

Abbie Tucker
Adam Macy
Alan Franks
Alice Aldridge
Alistair Lloyd
Amy Franks
Annabelle Schrivener
Annette Turner
Ben Archer
Bert Fry
Brenda Tucker
Brian Aldridge
Bunty and Reg Hebden
Caroline Sterling
Christine Barford
Christopher Carter
Clarrie Grundy
Clive Horrobin
Daniel Hebden Lloyd
David Archer
Debbie Aldridge
Deepak Gupta
Ed Grundy
Eddie Grundy
Elizabeth Pargetter
Emma Grundy
Fallon Rogers
Freda Fry
George Grundy
Graham Ryder

Hayley Tucker
Hazel Woolley
Heather Pritchard
Helen Archer
Ian Craig
Izzy Blake
Jack Woolley
James Bellamy
Jamie Perks
Jennifer Aldridge
Jill Archer
Jim Lloyd
Joe Grundy
Jolene Perks
Josh Archer
Kate Madikane
Kathy Perks
Kenton Archer
Kirsty Miller
Lewis Carmichael
Leon
Lilian Bellamy
Lily and Freddie Pargetter
Lorna
Lucas Madikane
Lynda Snell
Mabel Thompson
Marshall Latham
Matt Crawford
Maurice Horton

Mike Tucker
Neil Carter
Neville and Nathan Booth
Nic Hanson
Nigel Pargetter
Oliver Sterling
Pat Archer
Peggy Woolley
Phil Archer
Phoebe Aldridge
Pip Archer
Rachel Dorsey
Robert Snell
Roy Tucker
Ruairi Donovan
Ruth Archer
Sabrina and Richard Thwaite
Satya Khanna
Shula Hebden Lloyd
Sid Perks
Stephen Chalkman
Susan Carter
Tom Archer
Tony Archer
Usha Franks
Vicky Tucker
Wayne Tucson
William Grundy

Some can also be found under 'Silent Characters'

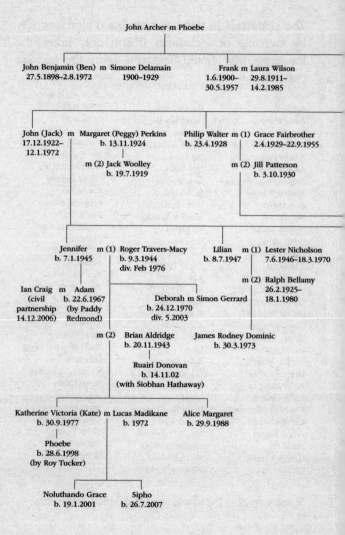

John Archer m Phoebe

John Benjamin (Ben) m Simone Delamain
27.5.1898–2.8.1972   1900–1929

Frank m Laura Wilson
1.6.1900–   29.8.1911–
30.5.1957   14.2.1985

John (Jack) m Margaret (Peggy) Perkins
17.12.1922–   b. 13.11.1924
12.1.1972

m (2) Jack Woolley
b. 19.7.1919

Philip Walter m (1) Grace Fairbrother
b. 23.4.1928   2.4.1929–22.9.1955

m (2) Jill Patterson
b. 3.10.1930

Jennifer m (1) Roger Travers-Macy
b. 7.1.1945   b. 9.3.1944
div. Feb 1976

Lilian m (1) Lester Nicholson
b. 8.7.1947   7.6.1946–18.3.1970

m (2) Ralph Bellamy
26.2.1925–
18.1.1980

Ian Craig m Adam
(civil   b. 22.6.1967
partnership (by Paddy
14.12.2006) Redmond)

Deborah m Simon Gerrard
b. 24.12.1970
div. 5.2003

m (2) Brian Aldridge
b. 20.11.1943

James Rodney Dominic
b. 30.3.1973

Ruairi Donovan
b. 14.11.02
(with Siobhan Hathaway)

Katherine Victoria (Kate) m Lucas Madikane
b. 30.9.1977   b. 1972

Alice Margaret
b. 29.9.1988

Phoebe
b. 28.6.1998
(by Roy Tucker)

Noluthando Grace   Sipho
b. 19.1.2001   b. 26.7.2007

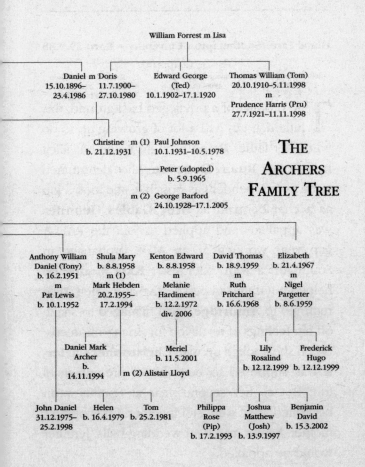

William Forrest m Lisa

Daniel m Doris
15.10.1896–
23.4.1986
11.7.1900–
27.10.1980

Edward George
(Ted)
10.1.1902–17.1.1920

Thomas William (Tom)
20.10.1910–5.11.1998
m
Prudence Harris (Pru)
27.7.1921–11.11.1998

Christine m (1) Paul Johnson
b. 21.12.1931
10.1.1931–10.5.1978

Peter (adopted)
b. 5.9.1965

m (2) George Barford
24.10.1928–17.1.2005

THE
ARCHERS
FAMILY TREE

Anthony William
Daniel (Tony)
b. 16.2.1951
m
Pat Lewis
b. 10.1.1952

Shula Mary
b. 8.8.1958
m (1)
Mark Hebden
20.2.1955–
17.2.1994

Kenton Edward
b. 8.8.1958
m
Melanie
Hardiment
b. 12.2.1972
div. 2006

David Thomas
b. 18.9.1959
m
Ruth
Pritchard
b. 16.6.1968

Elizabeth
b. 21.4.1967
m
Nigel
Pargetter
b. 8.6.1959

Daniel Mark
Archer
b.
14.11.1994

Meriel
b. 11.5.2001

m (2) Alistair Lloyd

Lily
Rosalind
b. 12.12.1999

Frederick
Hugo
b. 12.12.1999

John Daniel
31.12.1975–
25.2.1998

Helen
b. 16.4.1979

Tom
b. 25.2.1981

Philippa
Rose
(Pip)
b. 17.2.1993

Joshua
Matthew
(Josh)
b. 13.9.1997

Benjamin
David
b. 15.3.2002

ALICE ALDRIDGE

Home Farm/Southampton University • Born 29.9.88
(Hollie Chapman)

The product of a privileged background, this little rich girl had a lot of growing up to do when her father **Brian** brought home her illicit half-brother **Ruairi Donovan**. Alice determined to be as independent as possible: she took a job as a chambermaid at **Grey Gables** (**Jennifer** was appalled) and applied to join the RAF. A gap year working at an AIDS orphanage in South Africa with elder sister **Kate Madikane** helped put things in perspective and when Alice returned to **Ambridge** she'd managed to shake off her feelings of revulsion for Brian's misdeeds. When she hooked up with **Christopher Carter**, it was supposed to be a bit of pre-university fun. But as her second year at Southampton beckoned, they were still together. Christopher's mother, **Susan**, can hear wedding bells. Jennifer would be appalled.

BRIAN ALDRIDGE

Home Farm • Born 20.11.43
(Charles Collingwood)

Brian has sailed close to the wind in the past but **Jennifer** always managed to forgive his affairs, partly for the comfortable life he has been able to give her. But when Brian's mistress Siobhan Hathaway bore him **Ruairi Donovan** and then tragically died, leaving him to care for his son, the Aldridge marriage seemed doomed. Brian's relationship with his other children suffered too. Jennifer was forced to threaten divorce before Brian gave step-son and daughter **Adam Macy** and **Debbie Aldridge** management control of **Home Farm**. With a small child to raise, Jennifer was delighted to have a retired husband to share the burden. Retirement, alas, is not Brian's natural state. But at least the new chairman of **Borchester Land** gained some brownie points by helping to sort out his mother-in-law, **Peggy Woolley**'s finances and tolerating his sister-in-law, **Lilian Bellamy**, seeking refuge at Home Farm.

DEBBIE ALDRIDGE

(née Travers-Macy, formerly Gerrard)
Home Farm • Born 24.12.70
(Tamsin Greig)

In some ways Debbie used to be closer to her step-father **Brian Aldridge** than her mother **Jennifer** was. But Debbie is a straight arrow and Brian's affairs – reminding Debbie horribly of her own failed marriage to adulterer Simon Gerrard – severed the ties that once bound them so warmly. Debbie's farm management skills are much in demand. Joint manager of **Home Farm** with brother **Adam Macy**, she also manages the **Estate**'s arable land and a Hungarian dairy farm for a consortium in which Brian has an interest. Happy to keep a safe distance from Brian, she spends most of her time in Hungary, and it was there that she met her boyfriend, fellow farm manager **Marshall Latham**.

JENNIFER ALDRIDGE

(née Archer, formerly Travers-Macy)
Home Farm • Born 7.1.45
(Angela Piper)

Jennifer put her early career as a teacher and writer on hold to devote herself to her family. Pregnant by a local farm hand, unmarried Jennifer gave birth to **Adam** (now **Macy**) in 1967. She later married Roger Travers-Macy, who adopted Adam. They had a daughter **Debbie**, but the marriage didn't last and Jennifer wed **Brian** in 1976. More daughters followed: **Kate** (now **Madikane**) and **Alice**. Jennifer thought she had finished her parenting and, naturally enough, endured much torment before agreeing to take Brian's illegitimate child **Ruairi Donovan** into her home. Jennifer is not as soft as she sounds, however. She's **Peggy Woolley**'s daughter, all right, though her resilience was severely tested as she struggled to support Peggy with demented husband **Jack** as well as helping sister **Lilian** through turbulent times with and without her beloved **Matt Crawford**.

PHOEBE ALDRIDGE

Willow Farm • Born 28.6.98

(Scarlett Wakelin)

At first sight, you'd naturally assume that **Hayley Tucker** was Phoebe's mother, but the differing surnames tell the real story. Phoebe's real mum is in fact **Kate Madikane**, who in her hippy days had an incongruous relationship with clean-cut **Roy Tucker** and who now lives in Johannesburg. Phoebe was born in a tepee at the Glastonbury Festival. In Roy and Hayley's care, the bulk of her upbringing has been less colourful, if rather more stable. She's now at **Borchester** Green. Yes, the secondary school! It doesn't seem five minutes since Phoebe was being christened in a New Age ceremony on Lakey Hill. She was delighted at the arrival of her new sister **Abbie Tucker**, and they make a lovely, close family, cheerfully coping with the unpredictable occasional visits of exotic 'Mummy Kate'.

Everybody's image of a traditional English village is probably not a million miles from Ambridge. Village green with duck pond? Check. Village Hall? Check. Half-timbered pub? Check (**The Bull**). **Village Shop**? Check (just about). Ludicrously priced thatched cottages, unsympathetic modern infill and early morning departures by grey-faced commuters? Check, check and check. Gorgeous views and rubbish bus service? Checkity check. But this icon of traditionalism is trying to play its part in the very 21st-century fight against global climate change. Thanks to the leadership of **Pat Archer**, in 2008 Ambridge became one of the UK's 'transition communities'. Those unsympathetic developments may also be fewer in future thanks to **Matt Crawford** and partner-in-crime **Stephen Chalkman**'s removal from **Borchester Land**.

Nine holes spread across 20 acres, the course was part of **Grey Gables** until 2006 when it was sold to **Borchester Land**, along with the country park. **Leigh Barham**, the Director of Golf, is highly regarded as a charming man. The other staff include Susan Myers and **Kathy Perks**, who became clubhouse catering manager in April 2008 and finds the job far more hectic than she expected. A good lunch is expected by members. Indeed it's the main attraction for **Jennifer Aldridge**, who was sometimes dragged along by sister **Lilian** in more carefree times. Jennifer's husband **Brian** prefers shooting birds to putting balls, and Lilian's partner **Matt Crawford** has been rather bunkered of late.

AMBRIDGE HALL

*'… Are you seeking a short break in the heart of the English countryside? Look no further than our charming guesthouse! All rooms planned by myself, hostess **Lynda Snell**, in accordance with the principles of Feng Shui. All our breakfasts are locally sourced, of course. Special diets and allergies catered for with understanding and sympathy. I am myself a martyr to hay fever, and have created a low-allergen area of our extensive gardens as an elegant refuge for we sneezers and snufflers! Guests of a literary bent will be intrigued by our Shakespearean plot, using only plants named by the Bard! And visitors of all ages (well-behaved children are of course welcome) cannot fail to be delighted by our trio of llamas in the adjacent paddock…'*

Entry on the **Ambridge** village website.

AMBRIDGE ORGANICS

Harcourt Road, Borchester

Not a 'farm shop' exactly, as they are usually on the farm itself, but the 'farm's shop' – **Bridge Farm**'s, that is. Ambridge Organics is owned by **Pat** and **Tony Archer** and managed by their daughter **Helen**, employing **silent** Anja and **Kirsty Miller**, former girlfriend of Helen's brother **Tom**. The shop provides an ethical alternative to **Underwoods** food hall, selling Bridge Farm veg, yoghurt and ice cream, Helen's **Borsetshire** Blue cheese, plus a whole range of bought-in organic produce. Tom's sausages, too. Helen's wayward lodger, **Annette Turner**, has been known to put her undoubted talents as a saleswoman at the shop's disposal.

BEN ARCHER

Brookfield Farm • Born 15.3.02

(Thomas Lester)

When **Ruth** became pregnant with Ben it was a double blessing, coming as it did after her recovery from breast cancer. Ruth and **David** have to remind themselves of this when their 'blessed' offspring is fighting with his elder siblings **Josh** and **Pip**, or causing the sort of havoc that energetic children are prone to do.

DAVID ARCHER

Brookfield Farm • Born 18.9.59
(Timothy Bentinck)

Husband to **Ruth**, devoted father to **Pip**, **Josh** and **Ben**, parish councillor, deputy chair of the local NFU and stalwart of the **Ambridge** cricket team – he's just reached his half century. Having taken on **Brookfield Farm** in 2001 (much to the disgruntlement of squabbling siblings **Elizabeth Pargetter** and **Kenton**), it seemed like a good idea to recruit specialist herdsman Sam Batton to maximise the revenue from the expanded dairy herd. But in 2006 David's former fiancée Sophie Barlow reappeared. David spurned her advances too late to stop unhappy Ruth nearly sleeping with Sam. With both third parties off the scene, David worked hard to rebuild his marriage and the farm. If you need to know about the paddock grazing system, he's your man. He's also building a strong relationship with Pip, encouraging her interest in barn owls and even enduring her eco-friendly food fads.

HELEN ARCHER

Above the Village Shop• Born 16.4.79

(Louiza Patikas)

For a while, two bereavements caused **Pat** and **Tony Archer**'s daughter significant psychological problems. Her elder brother John died in an accident in 1998 and her partner Greg Turner committed suicide in 2004. Helen's attempts to control her unhappy life led to anorexia and, in 2006, to uncontrolled drinking and partying. Time at a specialist clinic helped her recover from the former. Counselling helped her understand and control the latter. Just as she was beginning to enjoy living over the shop – the **Village Shop**, not her own **Ambridge Organics** – Greg's daughter **Annette Turner** turned up and Helen felt obliged to offer her a bed at her 'compact' flat. She has since assumed the role of disapproving, if motherly, landlady. At least the arrival of charming Aussie **Leon** reignited her love life – for the time being anyway.

JILL ARCHER

(née Patterson)
Glebe Cottage • Born 3.10.30
(Patricia Greene)

To the despair of feminists, Jill Archer would probably describe herself as a mother and retired farmer's wife. It may be defining her by the others in her life, but it is an entirely accurate label. In 2007 she and **Phil** celebrated their golden wedding anniversary, along the way raising **Kenton**, **Shula** (now **Hebden Lloyd**), **David** and **Elizabeth** (now **Pargetter**). Many villagers outside her immediate family have also benefited from her motherly instincts. But Jill herself would be the first to point out that 'caring' doesn't mean 'doormat'. She'll fight her corner fiercely on important family matters or wider issues such as hunting. She's a committed 'anti', as **Oliver Sterling** knows to his cost. He has felt the sting from this committed apiarist who is currently less concerned about foxes than the threat of disease to her bees.

JOSH ARCHER

Brookfield Farm • Born 13.9.97

(George Bingham)

David and **Ruth**'s middle child is growing up fast and adjusting to life at secondary school. Luckily, he has been joined at **Borchester** Green by plenty of friends from Loxley Barratt Primary. He is evidently developing his mother's liking for pizza. Whether his love of animals will survive his fast-approaching teenage years remains to be seen, but he has tried his hand at bell-ringing, having heard that you get paid for doing it at weddings. Josh and brother **Ben** had a whale of a time on their father David's 50th birthday in September 2009, helping to blindfold him and chortling happily in the back of the car while being driven round to **Lower Loxley** for a surprise family meal. Luckily, Ruth was at the wheel.

KENTON ARCHER

April Cottage • Born 8.8.58
(Richard Attlee)

Kenton has been going through a mid-life crisis. Another one. This time it's a tattoo on increasingly flabby flesh, nights out with 'the boys' and plans to transform the homely charms of **Jaxx Caff** into a sophisticated bar for affluent young professionals. Kenton's partner, **Kathy Perks**, has always been grateful for the stalwart support he gave her during the traumatic trial of the man who raped her. She's also conscious that Kenton makes a wonderful 'uncle' to her son **Jamie**. But she was relieved when Jaxx owner Mr Sandlands turned down Kenton's initial plans and remained resistant to Jim Lloyd's entreaties that her partner would make a great bar manager. When would she – and Jamie – ever see him? His former waitress, **Emma Grundy**, knew the feeling, but her successor, the formidable Naomi, is far less accommodating. His daughter Meriel lives in New Zealand – only just far enough away, according to his ex-wife Mel.

PAT ARCHER

(née Lewis)
Bridge Farm • Born 10.1.52
(Patricia Gallimore)

Pat's been fighting for the environment most of her adult life. She and **Tony** converted **Bridge Farm** to organic as early as 1984 and Pat developed a thriving business processing their milk into yoghurt and ice cream. Although plodding Tony knows he's benefited from Pat's militant enthusiasm, there are times when he wishes for a quieter life. In 2008, Pat caused ructions by opposing close family members' plans for an anaerobic digester at **Home Farm**. Tony rightly predicted that the campaign would cause bad feeling for little effect. Having led the campaign to turn **Ambridge** into a transition community, Pat is now happily extolling the virtues of the new wetland water purification system at Bridge Farm. If only the lives of her surviving children **Helen** and **Tom** ran as smoothly.

PHIL ARCHER

Glebe Cottage • Born 23.4.28
(Norman Painting)

The 23rd of April is associated with three icons of England: Shakespeare, St George and Phil Archer. Through the 1960s and 1970s, Phil built up **Brookfield Farm**, finally passing it to son **David** and daughter-in-law **Ruth** in 2001. Still a staunch champion of their Hereford beef, he was out promoting it at the very last Royal Show. His marriage to **Jill** has been one of the most stable relationships in **Ambridge**. Only his attempts to commandeer the Aga have caused much tension between them. Phil sometimes overestimates his culinary skills, although his talents at the keyboard are still in demand at the church organ and the village-hall piano. He was happily passing on his passion for astronomy to grandson **Daniel Hebden Lloyd** until racier granddad **Jim Lloyd** began to divert the lad towards more earth-bound pleasures.

PIP ARCHER

Brookfield Farm • Born 17.2.93

(Helen Monks)

Pip is an earnest teenager who takes up causes with youthful passion. During Lent she would allow no food to pass her lips that had not been produced within a radius of five miles. More appealing to her father **David** has been her keen interest in observing barn owls. Mother **Ruth** appreciates her involvement with Brookfield's rational grazing system. In 2007, Pip joined Young Farmers and enthusiastically threw herself into activities from disco dancing to cattle judging. She also found a boyfriend, Jonathan. But her best friend, **Izzy Blake**, did not join her to do A levels at **Borchester** College, much to Pip's chagrin.

RUTH ARCHER

(née Pritchard)
Brookfield Farm • Born 16.6.68
(Felicity Finch)

In 2008, Ruth had a breast reconstruction, following a mastectomy because of cancer eight years earlier. It was the culmination of a tumultuous period, which could have seen Ruth's marriage to **David** blown apart by her – fortunately unconsummated – affair with the **Brookfield** herdsman Sam Batton. After Sam's departure, Ruth returned to her former role managing Brookfield's dairy herd while sharing with 'Dee-vid' the care of their children **Pip**, **Josh** and **Ben**. We can be sure that Ruth could have predicted very little of this in 1987 when she arrived at Brookfield as a fresh-faced agricultural student from Northumberland. No longer an outsider, she has nonetheless offered a sympathetic shoulder to other incomers. Her best friend is **Usha Franks**, despite the latter's contempt for Ruth's sister-in-law, **Shula**.

TOM ARCHER

1, The Green • Born 25.2.81

(Tom Graham)

It was only the intervention in 2005 of his hard-nosed uncle **Brian Aldridge** that saved Tom's over-extended organic sausage business. But their uneasy relationship soured when Brian did a deal with a supermarket behind his back. Prolonged arguments between uncle and nephew were only resolved when **Peggy Woolley** bought out Brian and bought in to Tom's organic business. The pigs are now back at **Bridge Farm** and Tom is back with **Brenda Tucker**. They had a major falling out when Tom was trying to cut a deal with **Matt Crawford** and Brenda didn't tell him the real reasons behind Matt's change of mind in offering to invest with him. She had overheard a conversation between **Stephen Chalkman** and Matt which indicated some financial misdealings, so Matt made the offer to shut her up. Tom bravely intervened when he caught Chalky threatening Brenda, and the couple are now engaged.

TONY ARCHER

Bridge Farm • Born 16.2.51
(Colin Skipp)

Tony could whinge for England. Only his nephew **Adam Macy** can match him for moaning about the frustrations of farming, albeit for different reasons. Tony is still pulling leeks by hand. No wonder he suffers from a bad back. But he keeps plugging away, committed to the organic cause like his wife **Pat**. At least he's now working for himself and his family since they bought the freehold of **Bridge Farm** from rapacious landlords **Borchester Land**. Does Tony ever cheer up? Well, yes, when he's taking a spin in his classic MG Midget. And he still enjoys a pint of Shires in **The Bull**, which offers endless opportunities to whinge about the size of his mortgage to anyone in earshot.

CHRISTINE BARFORD

(née Archer, formerly Johnson)
Woodbine Cottage • Born 21.12.31
(Lesley Saweard)

Phil **Archer**'s younger sister Chris – as she's always known in the family – lives a quiet retirement after many years running the riding stables (now owned by her niece **Shula Hebden Lloyd**) and two very different marriages. Peter, her adopted son from her first marriage, travels a lot as an administrator with a symphony orchestra. After the death of Peter's flaky father, Paul Johnson, Chris found more secure happiness with solid, dependable George Barford. But sadly George died in 2005 while they were waiting to re-occupy their house after a horrific firebomb attack. Arsonist **Clive Horrobin** was targeting his long-time enemy: gamekeeper and former policeman George. He was sentenced to 12 years, but it wasn't much comfort to Chris, who had to face life as a widow for the second time. In 2008, she became a churchwarden at **St Stephen's**.

JAMES BELLAMY

Born 30.3.1973
(Roger May)

Lilian **Bellamy**'s prodigal son moved slickly out of the London property market and into management consultancy just before the crash. In 2009 he made one of his rare visits to **Ambridge**, ostensibly to take 'Ma' out to dinner on her birthday and cheer her up. Against her expressed wishes, however, he made an unscheduled visit to The Dower House to warn **Matt Crawford** off shedding her assets to pay off his debts. The last thing James wants is to see his inheritance disappearing down a Matt-sized hole.

LILIAN BELLAMY

(née Archer, formerly Nicholson)
The Dower House • Born 8.7.47
(Sunny Ormonde)

What a year it has been for the former good-time 'girl' with a taste for toy boys and gin. Apparently tamed by her 'Tiger', **Matt Crawford**, she was briefly transformed from his pussycat to his tiger-skin rug – to be walked all over while he fretted over his forthcoming fraud trial. Not normally one of life's victims, Lilian finally cracked when her lover abandoned her by the side of a motorway. At the insistence of her sister **Jennifer Aldridge**, she sought asylum at **Home Farm**. Even her brother-in-law **Brian** showed glimmers of sympathy after she astonished him by turning down his offer to top up her glass. But Lilian and Matt were reunited at the Dower House after she found him down and almost out in the bar at **Grey Gables**. Like Tammy Wynnette, she seemed determined to stand by her man.

IZZY BLAKE

Meadow Rise, Borchester • Born 1993
(Lizzie Wofford)

Izzy could have gone to **Borchester** College with best friend **Pip Archer**. She scraped five GCSE grade Cs and one grade B in RE. But the grind of A levels doesn't appeal to this bright but sometimes wayward lass who once shocked Pip to the core by announcing that she was pregnant – a false alarm, as it turned out. Izzy wants to earn some instant money to pay for all those hooped earrings and crop tops. Above all, she just wants to get away from school. So she's following in mother's footsteps and working on a supermarket checkout. For Pip and her, this could be the parting of the ways – unless, that is, Izzy invests some of her wages on rejoining Young Farmers. Unlikely.

NEVILLE AND NATHAN BOOTH

Neville born 1949
Ambridge

Bell-ringer Neville Booth has attracted a surprising amount of unwarranted controversy over the years. When **Jolene Perks** (then Rogers) took advantage of **Kathy**'s absence to have a night of illicit passion with **Sid**, she parked her car away from **The Bull**. Unfortunately word got around that she'd appeared to spend the night at Mr Booth's house! More recently, **Bert Fry** described Neville as a 'Casanova in casual shoes' in the mistaken belief that he was making a play for **Freda**. Neville's nephew Nathan has a rather more deserved reputation for unpleasantness. Someone should have told him that when you've been caught cheating in a nettle-eating contest (he numbed his mouth with ice cubes), your chances of election to the parish council are slim. 'Slimy' is the word most often used to describe him.

BORCHESTER

Although **Felpersham** provides most of what passes for the bright lights in **Borsetshire**, this market town also has much to offer. Six miles north-east of **Ambridge**, Borchester still retains a historic core, with its clock tower and wool market. Shops include **Underwoods** department store and **Ambridge Organics**. Mental recreation is catered for by the Theatre Royal and multiplex cinema (well, all right, three screens) and more physical pursuits by the gym and swimming pool at the municipal leisure centre. And then you can throw all that good work away in many pubs, restaurants and cafes, including, of course, **Jaxx Caff**, managed (sort of) by the indefatigable **Kenton Archer**.

BORCHESTER LAND

Matt **Crawford** described it as 'the niftiest bit of footwork I've seen in 40 years in the business'. (This from a man with more tricks in his boots than Cristiano Ronaldo.) But **Brian Aldridge** knew better than to take it as a compliment. Usurping Matt's role as chairman of BL has had consequences far beyond the boardroom. Chief fellow conspirator was **Annabelle Schrivener**, the company lawyer, who believed that Matt's impending court case could damage the good name of BL. 'What good name?' might be the reaction from many **Ambridge** residents. The company still owns the Berrow **Estate**, whose 1,020 arable acres are managed by **Debbie Aldridge**. **Will Grundy** is back in charge of the pheasant shoot, one of Brian's pet projects. Other assets include the business units at Sawyer's Farm, although they have now sold the luxury housing development **Grange Spinney**.

BORSETSHIRE

Borsetshire is not exactly a real land re-labelled, like Hardy's Wessex, but it has a lot in common with the counties of Warwickshire and Worcestershire to the south and south-west of Birmingham. This attractive rural area is dominated to the east by the cathedral city and administrative centre of **Felpersham**. The second largest settlement is the market town of **Borchester**. **Ambridge** lies south-east of the Hassett Hills and falls under South Borsetshire District Council. The main local newspapers are the *Felpersham Advertiser* and the *Borchester Echo*, although the upstart *Westbury Courier* is making a name for itself with stunts and promotions. The area also has its own radio station named, with impressive clarity, Radio Borsetshire.

BRIDGE FARM

STOCK

92 milkers (Friesians) • 45 followers (heifers/calves)
45 fattening pigs

CROPS

115 acres grassland • 15 acres barley • 20 acres wheat
5 acres potatoes • 4 acres carrots • 2 acres leeks
3 acres swedes • 2 acres Dutch cabbage
1 acre Savoy cabbage • 5 acres mixed vegetable and
salad crops, including two poly-tunnels

LABOUR

Tony Archer • **Pat Archer** • **Tom Archer**
Helen Archer • **Jazzer** (part-time, pigs)
Clarrie Grundy (dairy)

Tony and **Pat Archer** now own the freehold to the 140 acres they once rented from the Estate, with an extra 32 acres from other landlords. Bridge Farm converted to organic in 1984. The farm's produce – including cheese, yoghurt and ice cream made in their own dairy – is sold through a wholesaler and to local outlets including **Ambridge Organics**. **Tom** has brought all his pigs back on site since the bust-up with **Brian**. Colin Kennedy has retired from the dairy.

BROOKFIELD FARM

STOCK

180 milkers (Friesians) • 79 followers (heifers/calves –
some Brown Swiss cross) • 85 beef cattle (Herefords)
325 ewes • Hens (small scale)

CROPS

339 acres grassland • 88 acres cereals • 10 acres
oilseed rape • 10 acres potatoes • 12 acres beans
10 acres forage maize

LABOUR

David Archer (managing)
Ruth Archer (managing and herdsperson)
Eddie Grundy (relief herdsperson)
Bert Fry (retired, casual) • Biff (sheepdog)

Brookfield is a 469-acre mixed farm incorporating the old holdings of Marney's and Hollowtree. After **Phil**'s retirement in 2001, **David** and **Ruth** contracted out the arable work to **Home Farm** and expanded the dairy herd. Their new paddock grazing system makes the grass more productive in terms of milk yield. High-quality beef from the Herefords is sold online and at the farm gate, and the lamb is marketed co-operatively under the Hassett Hills brand.

THE BULL

George Orwell once described a mythical perfect pub: The Moon Under Water. We think he'd like a lot of **Ambridge**'s only remaining local. A half-timbered building near the Village Green, The Bull offers excellent Shires ales, genial bar service from **Sid Perks** (usually) and his statuesque wife **Jolene** (almost always), as well as **Freda Fry**'s homely food. It still retains the traditional two bars, one being called the Ploughman's. Darts, skittles and boules are played, and there's even a pet peacock, Eccles, in the beer garden. However, Mr Orwell might be bemused by the small cyber area with two internet-linked computers. He'd certainly blanch at the music nights which **Fallon Rogers** organises in the upstairs function room. And we're sure he'd think the big screen, deployed for major sporting events, was far too redolent of Big Brother.

LEWIS CARMICHAEL

Lower Loxley Hall
(Robert Lister)

Everyone agreed that Lewis, suave and likable as he is, deserved more than a mere six months with **Nigel Pargetter**'s mother Julia, but sadly her death in November 2005 brought their happy marriage (the second for each of them) to a sudden end. Although retired, architect Lewis still does the occasional job that interests him, most recently the deceptively tricky extension and division of the house at **Willow Farm** into two dwellings. It leaves him plenty of time to lend a hand at **Lower Loxley**, running the art gallery or even (brave man) looking after the Pargetter twins, **Lily and Freddie**.

CHRISTOPHER CARTER

Ambridge View • Born 22.6.88

(William Sanderson-Thwaite)

Like his father **Neil**, Chris is a keen cricketer and a bell-ringer. He sounded the death knell for **Susan**'s hopes that at least one Carter would gain a degree when he announced in 2004 that he wanted to pursue a career as a farrier. But Neil was delighted when **Ronnie** took his son on. Chris successfully completed the four-year training scheme and his developing musculature made him a popular visitor to the area's stables and riding schools. Once Chris had letters after his name, Susan realised how proud she was of him. She also relished her son's close proximity to the horse-owning classes, even though he dumped the Lord Lieutenant's niece Venetia Streatfield to go out with a part-time barmaid. In the summer of 2008 he took up with another 'posh totty': **Alice Aldridge**. And they're still 'an item', despite Alice being a resident of Southampton during university term time.

NEIL CARTER

Ambridge View • Born 22.5.57

(Brian Hewlett)

Neil lives 'above the shop', which for him is a house he built himself on eight acres near **Willow Farm**. Indeed, he recently put another £5,000 on the mortgage. Not for a new conservatory, but to cover unpaid bills and clear debts on his pig business. Neil and pigs understand one another. It's taken his wife **Susan** some time to understand that he was never cut out for an office job. Luckily, his herd of Gloucester Old Spots is organic. It meant that **Tom Archer** could ask him to supply 30 weaners a month – a business move that may yet save Neil's bacon. Normally easygoing (some would say staid), bell-ringer Neil is tower captain at **St Stephen's** and ran the mobile belfry at the village fete. Reluctantly, he has come to accept that his daughter **Emma** is happier with **Ed Grundy** than with Ed's brother **Will**.

SUSAN CARTER

(née Horrobin)
Ambridge View • Born 10.10.63
(Charlotte Martin)

Nobody needs to buy the *Borchester Echo* at the **Village Shop** because Susan supplies all the local gossip. The shop manager and postmistress also supplies villagers with items valued for convenience rather than price. She is married to **Neil** and shared his worries over the future of his pig business. Susan has known hard times before on the rocky road away from childhood as one of the infamous **Horrobins**. She even went to prison in 1993 when forced to shelter her fugitive criminal brother **Clive**. It was a major setback for an Olympic-class social climber who still dreams that her son **Christopher** could marry **Alice Aldridge**. Daughter **Emma**, by contrast, gave her nightmares by marrying one Grundy and running off with another. At least she feels that **Ed Grundy** is shaping up to provide her daughter and grandson **George** with a better future.

CASA NUEVA

The gamekeeper's tied cottage at **Home Farm** is in quite an isolated spot, on a lane bordering Lyttleton Covert. **Will** and **Emma Grundy** returned from their Mexican honeymoon and named their home 'new house' in Spanish, hoping to lay to rest the ghost of the previous resident. Will's boss Greg Turner had committed suicide nearby. Sadly, the Curse of Greg could not be exorcised so easily, and the marriage was soon over. Perhaps, though, the sun is at last shining in the Casa. After a turbulent spell away from **Ambridge**, Will has found some happiness living in the heart of the woods for the second time with **Nic Hanson** and her children **Jake** and **Mia**.

STEPHEN CHALKMAN

Borchester
(Stephen Critchlow)

Stephen Chalkman is faced with the prospect of an even longer spell in 'choky' than his partner in crime, **Matt Crawford** – unless, of course, the court believes his claim that the dodgy deals were Matt's doing. At least Matt has pleaded guilty to fraudulent dealings. What's more, he stayed to face the music, unlike the sinister 'Chalky' who disappeared 'on holiday' when the Serious Fraud Office moved into **Ambridge**. He briefly reappeared to threaten **Brenda Tucker** to keep her 'trap' shut about what she may or may not have overheard in the office. Chalky is a former member of South **Borsetshire** District Council's planning committee; 'former' because he once neglected to mention his wife's involvement in a planning application which the committee was considering. The application subsequently became **Grange Spinney** and Chalkman became a director of **Borchester Land**, until he took leave of absence.

IAN CRAIG

Honeysuckle Cottage • Born 1970
(Stephen Kennedy)

As a gay man, Ian knows all about bigotry. **Ambridge** is hardly Brighton, but it must seem like a bastion of tolerance compared to his roots in rural Northern Ireland. With a few notable exceptions, like **Sid Perks**, most residents find this surprisingly easygoing chef good company when he's allowed out of the kitchens at **Grey Gables**. Perhaps because of his background, Ian tends to be more private about his homosexuality than civil partner Adam Macy and less comfortable about being 'out'. That sometimes puts a strain on their relationship. Ian has learnt from bitter experience that, rural England or rural Ireland, the bigotry never quite goes away.

MATT CRAWFORD

The Dower House • Born 7.8.47
(Kim Durham)

The prospect of spending anything up to ten years as a guest of Her Majesty does strange things to a man. And Matt's behaviour became very strange after the Serious Fraud Office came a-calling at The Dower House. His lover, **Lilian Bellamy**, stayed steely in his defence until he took to hurtling around the motorway system and staying in cheap motels off the upper reaches of the M6. She only moved out after he gave her the cold shoulder on the hard shoulder. And then it was only temporary. Once she'd heard what she wanted to hear – that he needed her by his side – she was right back in there. It seems a long time since Matt was the cocky chairman of **Borchester Land**. Lilian's 'Tiger' looks cornered.

RUAIRI DONOVAN

Home Farm • Born 14.11.02

(Matthew Rocket)

Ruairi is – in a word that 21st-century mores have made rather archaic – the illegitimate product of an extramarital affair between **Brian Aldridge** and the deceased Siobhan Hathaway (née Donovan). When Brian made the choice to stay with **Jennifer** rather than starting a new life with Siobhan, he imagined that his relationship with Ruairi (pronounced 'Rory') would be tenuous at best, especially when Siobhan moved to Germany. But her death from cancer in May 2007 brought the child – after mighty ructions – to **Home Farm**. Jennifer made heroic efforts and even Brian applied himself to hands-on fatherhood. Whether their work will compensate for the loss of Ruairi's real mother remains to be seen. At least he now has a memorial bench on which to sit and think about Siobhan when he's old enough.

RACHEL DORSEY

Felpersham
(Deborah McAndrew)

Rachel arrived as archdeacon of **Felpersham** diocese in 2007. Rachel and **Ambridge**'s vicar **Alan Franks** have a similar, modernising outlook and she soon encouraged him to embark on radical projects such as the proposal to remove the pews from **St Stephen's** – eventually narrowly rejected by the PCC. To the consternation of some of the more traditional parishioners, Rachel was very supportive of Alan's engagement to **Usha** (then Gupta) and in fact presided over one of their marriage services – the Christian one, naturally – in August 2008.

THE ESTATE

More correctly, the Berrow Estate: see **Borchester Land**.

FELPERSHAM

Birmingham lies some 30 miles from **Ambridge**, many of whose more recent arrivals commute there every day. But for most purposes the cathedral city of Felpersham fits the bill. Only 17 miles to the east of the village, the county town of **Borsetshire** is well stocked with shops, eating places and opportunities for night-time excess. It also has a football team, owned by the husband of image consultant Blaize Montpelier, a cathedral and a university. Among its alumni are **Roy Tucker** and, more recently, his sister **Brenda**.

ALAN FRANKS

The Vicarage, Ambridge
(John Telfer)

The vicar of **Ambridge**, Penny Hassett, Darrington and Edgeley is normally a hale and hearty character who roars around his parishes on a motorbike. But he finds himself treading on eggshells when dealing with former friend and ex-churchwarden **Shula Hebden Lloyd.** He is embarrassed that she now worships at **Felpersham** Cathedral, having made plain her opposition to the vicar marrying a Hindu. The first marital row between Alan and **Usha** came when his wife neglected to mention that she had let her former cottage to another of Shula's bête noires, her father-in-law **Jim Lloyd**. In other respects, the vicar and his missus seem happily married. She shares his love of motorbikes, but not his passion for bracing holidays under canvas, risking the vagaries of an English summer.

AMY FRANKS

The Vicarage/Manchester University • Born 1989
(Vinette Robinson)

Amy is of mixed race, the product of the Reverend **Alan's** first marriage to Catharine, who died in 1995. There are feisty genes on both sides of the family. Alan, a champion of social justice, isn't afraid of a fight and nor is Amy's grandmother **Mabel Thompson**. This led to fiery times in 2008, as Amy clashed with Mabel, who strongly opposed Alan's marriage to **Usha**. Amy is now in the third year of a midwifery degree at Manchester University, well away from her one-time best friend in **Ambridge**, **Alice Aldridge**, who is studying in Southampton. To be honest, the friendship had already been severely strained by Alice's attempt to join the RAF, a move significantly at odds with Amy's radical views.

USHA FRANKS

(née Gupta)
The Vicarage, Ambridge • Born 17.6.62
(Souad Faress)

Usha woke up on her first wedding anniversary in a luxury hotel. It must have seemed like paradise after the week she had endured in a tent, indulging husband **Alan**'s passion for the Great Outdoors. As Usha is a practising Hindu and Alan is the local vicar, joy was not totally unconfined when they married. **Shula Hebden Lloyd** resigned as churchwarden after her unguarded comments made the local paper (although there's history there: Shula had had an affair with an earlier boyfriend of Usha's). Usha's family struggled to accept the match and she received angry threats from within her own community, bringing back horrible memories of the racist attacks she'd suffered when she moved to **Ambridge** in 1991. Usha is a partner in **Felpersham** solicitors Jefferson Crabtree, a determined figure who showed true grit in limping across the line at the Felpersham Marathon.

BERT FRY

Brookfield Bungalow • Born 1936

(Eric Allan)

There came a man from out the West
Some farming for to try
He worked the land for many years
That man was stout Bert Fry.

*Retired from **Brookfield** late in life*
He still worked casually
But, gilet wearing, also guided
*Guests at **Lower Loxley**.*

A champion vintage ploughman
And, like John Clare long before,
Bert is a Ploughman Poet
(And to some a champion bore)

Churchgoing, cricket umpiring
No greater love has he
Than wife of over fifty years
*His much-beloved **Fre-(-da)***

FREDA FRY

Brookfield Bungalow

Freda has been the light of **Bert**'s life for over 50 years and, to use a little poetic licence, could well be the muse to inspire his passion for writing verse that makes William McGonagall seem like Seamus Heaney. She is also a renowned cook, running the food operation at **The Bull** with dedication and skill. Much to landlord **Sid**'s irritation, she didn't resent the intrusion of **Jolene**'s former husband **Wayne Tucson**. Indeed, she rather welcomed having a helping hand. Although Freda works in a pub (as well as cleaning the posh holiday home Arkwright Hall), Bert is careful that she doesn't drink there – at least no alcohol. We still don't know what happened, but as Bert will gnomically inform you, they can never go back to Filey.

GRANGE FARM

STOCK
30 milkers (Guernseys)

CROPS
50 acres grassland

LABOUR
Ed Grundy (tenant farmer)
Mike Tucker (dairy processing)

A working farm – although some may dispute that description – until the bankrupt **Grundys** were evicted in 2000. The bulk of the acreage was absorbed back into the **Estate** and the farmhouse sold with 50 acres to **Oliver Sterling**, who in 2006 established a small herd of Guernseys to supply **Mike Tucker**'s milk round. Oliver has now retired, and **Ed Grundy** has taken over the farm as tenant farmer. The herd is currently being expanded, Ed has rented more land from **Borchester Land** for grazing and Mike is planning to add more milk rounds.

GRANGE SPINNEY

After much controversy, this development of 12 luxury houses and six 'low-cost' homes was built by **Borchester Land** in 2003 on a few acres of former farmland. Many of the residents commute to Birmingham and elsewhere and don't play much part in the community. Notable exceptions are **Richard and Sabrina Thwaite**, who have thrown themselves into village life – even if Sabrina's fierce competitiveness has put a few **Ambridge** noses out of joint.

'...yes, **Jack**, Grey Gables Hotel. No, you don't own it any more, you sold it to **Caroline** and **Oliver Sterling**. Yes, Caroline used to be your manager there. Ooh, years and years. Now this is **Roy Tucker**. You remember Roy, he's deputy manager. Jean-Paul? No, he left years ago. The head chef's **Ian Craig** – the Irishman? Well, never mind. Come on, we're going to have a little swim at the health club. Golf? Maybe we could play a few holes tomorrow. No, you sold the club as well – to **Borchester Land**? Now this is – oh you know. Yes, **Lynda Snell**, the receptionist. Sorry Lynda, senior receptionist. Yes Jack, she's very memorable, I agree...'

Peggy Woolley overheard talking to her husband **Jack.**

CLARRIE GRUNDY

Keeper's Cottage • Born 12.5.54
(Rosalind Adams)

To **Eddie**'s credit, he once said that Clarrie wasn't behind him; she'd always been beside him. Figuratively speaking, that is. She's too busy trying to scrape a living to supplement Eddie's erratic earnings to be literally by his side. Clarrie works incessantly. Not only does she cook and clean for Eddie and 88-year-old father-in-law **Joe**, she also holds down two jobs, in the dairy at **Bridge Farm** and behind the bar at **The Bull**. On top of this, she is constantly trying to reconcile her two feuding sons **Ed** and **William**. To escape her daily drudgery, Clarrie likes a nice romantic novel and very occasionally escapes to Great Yarmouth to see her sister Rosie Mabbott. But her best-ever holidays have been very occasional trips to her beloved France. Eddie is not a natural francophile, but he is particularly keen on Clarrie in French knickers.

ED GRUNDY

Rickyard Cottage, Brookfield • Born 28.9.84
(Barry Farrimond)

There be Grundys again at **Grange Farm**. Well, one Grundy in particular, and he has been working there for some time as **Oliver Sterling**'s herd manager. The difference now is that Ed is running the show, since Oliver gave him the tenancy on very generous terms. What's more, he was already seeking to expand the herd and the grazing land. It looks as though he's determined to repay the faith that Oliver showed in him. This is a young man with a past. He's served community punishments for joyriding and burglary and once tried to grow cannabis in a barn at **Bridge Farm** with his mate **Jazzer McCreary**. Ed's had a complicated relationship with **Emma Grundy** – no, actually she's his former sister-in-law (we said it was complicated). They got back together in 2008, much to the dismay of Ed's brother and Emma's former hubby **Will**, whose son **George** lives with them.

EDDIE GRUNDY

Keeper's Cottage • Born 15.3.51

(Trevor Harrison)

While **Ed Grundy** was gearing up to become the official tenant at **Grange Farm**, his father Eddie was beginning to mellow and mature in a way that his home-made cider rarely has had chance to do. **David** and **Ruth Archer** evidently thought he was trustworthy enough to take over **Brookfield** for a week while they took the family on holiday. Quite a risk on their part, considering that Eddie's rather slipshod management techniques led to the loss of Grange Farm in the first place. Good job **Clarrie** was going to be around. Eddie certainly needed the work. His many rural enterprises (landscaping, composting and garden ornaments, to name but three) have been badly hit by the recession. And his more recent wheeze – trying to unearth valuable relics located by a metal detector – was as doomed as his hopes of making it big as a country and western singer.

EMMA GRUNDY

(née Carter)
Rickyard Cottage, Brookfield • Born 7.8.84
(Felicity Jones)

She may no longer be running **Jaxx Caff** during **Kenton**'s lengthy absences, but Emma is still trying to hold down two jobs while getting son **George** to and from his new school at Loxley Barratt. Delight when George's father, **Will Grundy**, agreed to help out turned to disapproval when Will's girlfriend **Nic Hanson** brought the lad home one afternoon. Emma has been suspicious of Nic since she once smacked George while struggling to cope with the demands of three boisterous children. More traditional listeners might agree with Emma's mother **Susan Carter** that she shouldn't be so precious. After all, she was the little hussy who set this complicated process in motion by running away from Will at an early stage in their marriage and setting up home with his brother **Ed**, causing ructions among the Carters and almost fratricide between the Grundy brothers.

GEORGE GRUNDY

Rickyard Cottage, Brookfield/Casa Nueva
Born 7.4.05
(Rui Thacker)

This little chap fitted more familial complications into his first year than many people have in their whole lives. He was named George after **William Grundy**'s former gamekeeping mentor George Barford and Edward after... well, who? Grandfather **Eddie**? Or Will's brother **Ed**, whom **Emma** mistakenly believed to be George's real father? A DNA test proved otherwise. Not much later Emma was divorced from Will and estranged for several years from Ed. Although resident with his mum, George spends regular time with Will and, rather more problematically with his girlfriend **Nic Hanson**. When Ed and Emma got back together, Will was so distraught that he had to leave the village, even though it meant seeing much less of his beloved son, who started primary school in September 2009.

JOE GRUNDY

Keeper's Cottage • Born 18.9.21

(Edward Kelsey)

Did you catch that tantalising whiff of liniment and home-made cider, with subtle top notes of horse manure and pipe tobacco? Joe Grundy's probably just passed by. Joe was forced into retirement when he lost **Grange Farm** through bankruptcy, and is delighted that grandson **Ed** has it back again. When his trap is not being pulled around the village by his pony Bartleby, Joe's content to potter around in the garden at Keeper's Cottage. He also keeps things tidy for **Kathy Perks** at April Cottage next door. Although he celebrated his 88th birthday not long ago, there's plenty of life left in this old dog. He's struck up an unlikely alliance with his new drinking mate **Jim Lloyd**, and in 2008 he enjoyed a brief friendship with Mildred Sommerskill, a visiting former resident. Sadly, this was short-lived. Mildred returned to Canada, where she died of cancer.

WILLIAM GRUNDY

Casa Nueva • Born 9.2.83

(Philip Molloy)

If you're the sort of person who likes taking risks, try telling Will Grundy to count his blessings. He has a lovely, healthy son, **George**, and a responsible job as a gamekeeper. Indeed, he returned to **Ambridge** bursting with new ideas for the shoot after a temporary exile in Gloucestershire. What's more, he was reunited with girlfriend **Nic Hanson**. Add to that the inheritance that enabled him to buy 1, The Green and rent it out, and Will should be as chirpy as a lark at daybreak. But he's never likely to forget that his marriage to George's mother was blown apart, thanks to **Emma**'s longing for Will's brother **Ed**. When Ed and Emma reunited in 2008, Will came close to strangling Ed before fleeing to the east coast. A brief brotherly rapprochement on the sand dunes did not survive their return to **Ambridge**.

GRUNDYS' FIELD

When **Lynda Snell** is showing her B&B guests round **Ambridge**, she's careful to avoid Grundys' Field. The scrappy pole barn, rough shed and old shipping container aren't the most picturesque sights, admittedly. **Eddie Grundy**'s decrepit tractor and digger don't help. And the gently stewing mounds of compost are hardly a tourist attraction either. But this 3.4 acres is the engine room of Eddie's business activities (very occasionally abetted by **Joe**). They don't just store their garden ornaments and materials for the landscaping business there. In the colder months they raise Christmas turkeys and over-winter sheep for hill farmers. Spring and summer see car-boot sales, with children entertained by the Berkshire sow Barbarella. And year round you should be able to get a pint of home-made cider, as long as you've a strong constitution and a disregard for the excise laws.

DR DEEPAK GUPTA

Tettenhall, Wolverhampton
(Madhav Sharma)

This doctor of medicine (now retired) was a Ugandan Asian who was forced by Idi Amin's expulsion in 1972 to move his family to Britain. Disapproving of his daughter **Usha**'s settling in **Ambridge**, he and his depressive wife kept their distance for many years, letting his sister-in-law **Satya Khanna** and son Shiv be Usha's link to the family. But this changed in 2008 when Usha received threats following her engagement to **Alan Franks**. Perhaps engineered by cunning Satya, Dr Gupta turned up in Ambridge unannounced. Despite a difficult few days, this patrician traditionalist was impressed by Alan's willingness to embrace a Hindu wedding ceremony as well as the planned Christian one. Returning to Wolverhampton, he managed to persuade Mrs Gupta to accept the union.

NICOLA (NIC) HANSON

Casa Nueva • Born 1980
(Becky Wright)

Will second time around prove luckier for Nic? Time will tell. But she, Jake (5) and Mia (3) have settled in again at **Casa Nueva**, the gamekeeper's cottage. The keeper is **Will Grundy**, enjoying a new lease of life on the domestic front as well as at work. Last time the relationship ended in tears – Nic's mingling with those of Will's son **George**. The isolation of the woods and the difficulty of being in loco parentis during George's regular visits proved hard for Nic. Things came to a head when Will accused her of abuse after he caught her smacking the lad, although in Nic's defence it was after a tussle between George and Mia. Outraged, Nic flounced back to her mum's in **Borchester**. Will has since wooed her back and helped her pass her driving test. As a result, she's less dependent on an irregular rural bus service to get her out of the woods.

BUNTY AND REG HEBDEN

Bunty born 20.2.22
(Bunty – Sheila Allen)

Alistair Lloyd is in the unfortunate position of having an extra set of quasi in-laws – the grandparents of his adopted son **Daniel Hebden Lloyd**. Retired solicitor Reg and wife Bunty are the parents of **Shula**'s first husband Mark. Having had a bad experience in private education as a child, Alistair insisted that Daniel should go to the local state primary, against Reg and Bunty's wishes. But they won the second – and arguably most significant – round, siding with Shula and funding the boy through **Felpersham** Cathedral School since 2006.

HOLLERTON JUNCTION

Yes. I remember Hollerton —
The name, because one afternoon
(No seat!) the London train drew up there
Abruptly. It was late June.
The iPods hissed. Someone cleared his email.
No one left and no one came
On the bare platform. What I saw
Was Hollerton – only the name
*And '**Ambridge** – 6 miles', and grass,*
And Hassett Hills, and silage clamp,
And 'Services to Birmingham – Platform 2.
Wheelchair access via ramp.'
And for that minute a moped growled
Close by, and round him, noisier,
Farther and farther, all the cars
*Of **Borchester** and **Borsetshire**.*

With apologies to Edward Thomas.

HOME FARM

STOCK
280 ewes (early lambing) • 110 hinds, stags, calves

CROPS
1,124 acres cereals • 148 acres grassland
152 acres oil seed rape • 36 acres linseed
80 acres woodland • 10 acres willow (game cover)
4 acres strawberries • 6 acres maize

OTHER
25-acre riding course • Fishing lake • Maize maze

LABOUR
Adam Macy (managing) • **Debbie Aldridge** (managing)
Andy, Jeff (general workers) • **Brian Aldridge** (relief)
William Grundy (gamekeeper), Pete (assistant keeper)
Students and seasonal labour • Fly (sheepdog)

With 1,585 mainly arable acres, Home Farm is the largest in **Ambridge** and carries out contract farming for **Brookfield**, the **Estate** and other local farms. As a partner in the Hassett Hills Meat Company, it raises and supplies high-quality lamb to butchers and caterers, and sells its venison and strawberries at local farmers' markets.

CLIVE HORROBIN

A guest of Her Majesty • Born 9.11.72

(Alex Jones)

Many families have a black sheep. But when the family in question is the **Horrobins** then it gives a new dimension to the concept. Clive isn't prejudiced – he'll rob anyone, anywhere – but many of his illegal activities have been in the **Ambridge** area. These include an armed robbery on the **Village Shop**, after which he forced his big sister **Susan Carter** to harbour him (for which she served time); a string of burglaries on local homes; and – worst of all – a vicious vendetta against former policeman George Barford, which culminated in 2004 in a firebomb attack on George's house. Badly burned, Clive sought refuge with Susan once more, but this time she did the right thing. Clive got 12 years.

THE HORROBINS

6, The Green, and elsewhere

Some think the Horrobins' role in life is to make the Grundys look classy. They've certainly had a higher proportion of jailbirds: **Clive**, Keith and **Susan** (now **Carter**) have all done time, and while many felt that Susan's sentence was unwarranted, there was no such sympathy for her brothers. Unfortunate paterfamilias Bert Horrobin is a former road worker and his wife Ivy supplements her pension with cleaning work. Daughter Tracy flits from job to job and it's best not to ask how Gary and Stewart earn their beer money. Perhaps unsurprisingly, **Neil Carter** feels that 6, The Green isn't an ideal environment for the care of his grandson **George Grundy**, no matter how convenient it is occasionally for **Emma**.

MAURICE HORTON

Borchester
(Philip Fox)

Agrumpy man with a cleaver in his hand is perhaps not the most reassuring of figures, but butcher Maurice has much to be grumpy about. Having lost his wife, son and a previous business through compulsive gambling, Maurice was happy to give up a tottering one-man shop in **Felpersham** to work part-time at the business units at Sawyer's Farm. There he makes sausages for **Tom Archer**, supplementing this with work in a supermarket and butchering the occasional venison carcass for **Home Farm**. Despite Maurice's moody demeanour, **Alistair Lloyd** has much to be grateful to Maurice for. In fact, we'd say Alistair's in his debt, but that might be rather misleading, as Maurice is Alistair's sponsor at the **Borchester** branch of Gamblers Anonymous.

JAXX CAFF

Borchester

There's a corner of an English market town that is forever America. At least it must seem forever to manager **Kenton Archer** since he opened a café in **Borchester** with the sort of décor more commonly found in diners off Route 66 in the 1950s. The music is as retro as the surroundings. Elvis and the Everley Brothers feature prominently. Kenton has evidently heard rather more of this nostalgia-on-a-loop than he would like. He would prefer to spend less time serving and more time developing his plans to transform the place into a sophisticated café bar. Unfortunately for him, his assistant Naomi will not countenance his frequent absences, as the more indulgent **Emma Carter** once did. Nor did the new owner, Mr Sandlands, buy into his dreams initially. Could it be second time lucky for Kenton's revised plans?

SATYA KHANNA

Wolverhampton
(Jamila Massey)

Usha Franks's parents didn't want their daughter to move to the countryside, so for many years Auntie Satya was Usha's main link to the parental generation. Satya often used to descend when she sensed that Usha needed support, even if Usha didn't want it at the time – although the accompanying food parcels were always welcome, as Usha isn't a great cook. After numerous failed matchmaking attempts, you'd think Satya would have been pleased when Usha fell in love with a prominent, pious and professional man. Unfortunately that man was **Alan Franks**, the local vicar, which didn't go down at all well with this devout Hindu. Satya strongly opposed the wedding, until threats to Usha from within the Asian community aroused her protective nature. She became the prime mover in the Hindu end of Usha and Alan's wedding ceremonies in August 2008.

MARSHALL LATHAM

Hungary
(Paul Curran)

Debbie Aldridge's boyfriend made his first visit to meet her parents at **Home Farm** in May 2009. **Jennifer** had met him before, on a trip to visit Debbie in Hungary, and saw nothing to alter her first impressions that he is utterly charming. **Brian** is not so sure. Marshall is a bit too much of a new man for his liking. He makes his own jam, for goodness' sake. Marshall is a British farm manager running a UK-owned farm in Hungary but, unlike Debbie's enterprise, which has a large dairy herd, his is totally arable. Also unlike Debbie, Marshall is a first-generation farmer: his family in Hitchin, Hertfordshire, have no agricultural background.

LEON

(Nicholas Osmond)

Australian barman Leon chatted up **Helen** very quickly and the couple got together, in spite of Helen's reticence, because **Kirsty** gave Leon her mobile phone number. He's good looking and charming and a wow with the ladies. Helen needs someone in her life and so time will tell. Meanwhile, one of the other reasons Leon may stick around is that his paternal grandfather lives in England.

ALISTAIR LLOYD

The Stables
(Michael Lumsden)

Life never seems to get much better for Alistair, the village vet, despite apparently gaining control over his problems with gambling. At least he has the more wholesome pleasures of village cricket. Even that didn't seem much fun when **Adam Macy**'s win-at-all-costs mentality succeeded his more laid-back approach to captaining the **Ambridge** team. What's left of Alistair's spare time, after tending to the needs of all creatures great and small, is largely taken up by the far less predictable demands of his eccentric father, **Jim Lloyd**, since he became a full-time Ambridge resident. The retired history professor delights in winding up **Alistair**'s wife **Shula**, putting even more strain on family life at **The Stables**. There must be times when Alistair looks forward to being called out to a cow with a prolapsed uterus.

DANIEL HEBDEN LLOYD

The Stables • Born 14.11.94
(Dominic Davies)

The 'Hebden' part of Daniel's surname comes from his mother **Shula**'s first husband, Mark, who died in a car crash without knowing that his wife was pregnant. Mark's parents, **Bunty and Reg**, have funded Daniel's attendance at **Felpersham** Cathedral School, against the wishes of his father (by adoption) **Alistair**. The lad is now at an age when he can challenge his parents' assumptions in any number of areas. And he's being encouraged to do so by Alistair's father, **Jim**, who cited the need to see more of Daniel as one of his reasons for moving to **Ambridge**. The far more stable influence of Shula's father **Phil**, who shared his interest in astronomy with his grandson, could soon be waning like the moon in September.

JIM LLOYD

Blossom Hill Cottage

(John Rowe)

Ambridge's answer to Mr Toad zips around the by-ways of **Borsetshire** in a classic Riley, possibly with a sticker asking other drivers to 'honk if you speak Latin' on the back window. Having appeared on a plinth at the village fete as Marcus Porcius Cato, this retired academic seems determined to make the most of his final years. He moved to Ambridge to spend more time with his family. **Alistair** is not exactly overjoyed at being at his father's beck and call, and **Shula** found it very difficult to be civil to a militant atheist who mocks her religious beliefs. **Daniel** loves having him around, however – particularly since his adoptive grandfather allowed him a go at the wheel of the Riley (off road, of course). Jim is drawn to Ambridge's more buccaneering characters, notably Shula's twin brother **Kenton Archer**.

SHULA HEBDEN LLOYD

(formally Hebden, née Archer)
The Stables • Born 8.8.58
(Judy Bennett)

The growing strain in Shula's voice has two main sources. One is the close proximity of her mischievous father-in-law, **Jim Lloyd**. The other is the ongoing tension with vicar and former friend **Alan Franks** and his wife **Usha**. As she drives to **Felpersham** Cathedral on Sunday mornings, Shula must wonder whether her past sins are coming back to haunt her. She's still reaping the effects of her affair with **Usha**'s former partner, Richard Locke, in 1998. Ten years later, Shula resigned as churchwarden following unwise remarks to a reporter about the planned marriage of a Christian vicar to a Hindu – another blow to her reputation as the solid twin to flaky **Kenton Archer**. Shula runs a riding school and stables and is married to **Alistair Lloyd**. Her first husband Mark was killed in a car crash in 1994, unaware that after infertility treatment Shula was pregnant with **Daniel**.

LORNA

(Alison Belbin)

Lorna took over **Kathy Perks'** old job as Café and Shop Manager at **Lower Loxley** in 2008. She is **Emma Grundy**'s boss there. She helped with the make-up at the village panto at Christmas. She has a great sense of humour and joined Kathy in an April Fool joke against **Kenton**. "No Kenton, your tattoo does not say 'Lucky in every endeavour'; it says 'closed for cleaning!'."

LOWER LOXLEY HALL

'A great day out for all the family!' claim the flyers and indeed this impressive mansion with extensive parkland has much to offer; quite a lot of it spawned by the passing enthusiasms of its owner **Nigel Pargetter** (one of the reasons his wife **Elizabeth** indulges them). Nigel runs falconry courses and displays with falconer Jessica; the grounds boast rare breeds, cycle trails, an art gallery, a tree-top walk and vines producing Lower Loxley's own wine. He's also a keen horseman; the annual point-to-point was supplemented in 2008 by a gung-ho team chase. And, with its more sober hat on, Lower Loxley welcomes conferences, weddings and other functions – especially with a 'green' tinge. Staff include ancient retainers Edgar and Eileen Titcombe, volunteer guide **Bert Fry**, retail and catering manager **Lorna** and Hugh the Orangery Café's chef. **Hayley Tucker** runs activity visits for schoolchildren, and **Emma Grundy** works in the Orangery as a waitress.

ADAM MACY

Honeysuckle Cottage • Born 22.6.67
(Andrew Wincott)

Adam's competitive streak has come to the fore – worryingly for his civil partner **Ian Craig** and excruciatingly for fellow members of the **Ambridge** Cricket Club. After wresting control from captain **Alistair Lloyd**, he embarked on the uphill task of getting them fit and focused on winning. Success is important to Adam on the cricket field and, even more so, on the farm. Despite his profitable innovations, including a thriving soft-fruit business, Adam has an uneasy relationship with step-father **Brian Aldridge**. Brian would deny it, but he has difficulties with Adam being gay. **Jennifer** has been fiercely protective of her son, who was conceived with a cowman called Paddy Redmond and later adopted by her first husband Roger Travers-Macy. In 2008, under severe threats from Jennifer, Brian made Adam and his half-sister **Debbie** joint managers of the farm, with a generous profit share.

KATE MADIKANE

(née Aldridge)
Johannesburg • Born 30.9.77
(Kellie Bright)

Was the former hippy becoming restless again? That's the impression **Debbie Aldridge** came away with after her latest trip to South Africa to visit her stepsister and her family. Could it be that Kate is missing **Ambridge** or, more likely, her daughter **Phoebe**, who now lives happily with her father, **Roy Tucker**, stepmother **Hayley** and half-sister **Abbie**? At the height of Kate's wild teenage days (expelled from school, stealing from home, disappearing with travellers...), **Jennifer** and **Brian** must have despaired of their daughter ever settling down into respectable domesticity. When she eventually did, it was in Johannesburg with a black South African (**Lucas**), rather than in Edgeley with a nice Young Farmer. Kate's children with Lucas are daughter Noluthando (born 2001) and son Sipho (born 2007). She works as a volunteer in an AIDS orphanage.

LUCAS MADIKANE

Johannesburg • Born 1972
(Connie M'Gadzah)

Cynics would say that **Kate** getting pregnant by a black South African was just another ploy to shock the more conservative elements in **Ambridge** (it certainly didn't go down well with her grandmother **Peggy Woolley**). But the match survived their move from the pleasant surroundings of Cape Town to the more challenging environment of Johannesburg when journalist Lucas took a job with the South African Broadcasting Corporation. Lucas married Kate in June 2001 and has proved to be a calming influence on her.

JAZZER MCCREARY

Meadow Rise, Borchester • Born 1984
(Ryan Kelly)

The rasping Glaswegian brogue of Jack 'Jazzer' McCreary brings a bracing injection of big-city cockiness to small-town and village life in middle England. Some women are evidently impressed by it, like **Annette Turner** and the bored young wives who look forward to his early-morning delivery (Jazzer is an archetypal milkman, among other things). But, as Annette has discovered, he hates to be tied down. Romantic he is not, although he does carry a torch for 'that wee lassie' who used to do the pigs for **Tom Archer** (Hannah, who has since returned to university). Jazzer is a pig man as well as a milkman, and a roadside and car-boot salesman, too. The wonder is that he has any energy left for clubbing, let alone anything else. It is to be hoped that he's taking fewer chemical stimuli than he did in a feral youth spent joyriding, housebreaking and cannabis growing in the company of **Ed Grundy**.

KIRSTY MILLER

Borchester
(Anabelle Dowler)

Chirpy Kirsty hasn't been desperately lucky with men in recent years. Her six-year on-off relationship with **Tom Archer** ended in 2005 when he fell for someone else – only for Tom to be dumped himself soon after he'd given Kirsty the 'big E'. While Tom eventually fell for her best mate **Brenda Tucker**, Kirsty took up with the **Brookfield** herdsman Sam Batton. She was keen; he was cooling fast, having fallen for **Ruth Archer** (but that's another kettle of rancid fish). At least Kirsty didn't let the break-up with Tom sour her job at the family's shop **Ambridge Organics**, where she works for Tom's sister **Helen**. Tom and Kirsty have managed to bury their past and are on good terms now when they meet at the shop or when she's working part-time at **The Bull**.

ELIZABETH PARGETTER

(née Archer)
Lower Loxley Hall • Born 21.4.67
(Alison Dowling)

Elizabeth might be the youngest of **Phil** and **Jill Archer**'s children but my goodness she can punch above her weight, especially when she thinks she's getting less than her fair share. Husband **Nigel** can sometimes be embarrassed by 'Lizzie's' doggedness, but **Lower Loxley** has undoubtedly benefited from the combination of his old-world eccentricity and her pugilistic nature. Before her marriage to Nigel, Elizabeth had an abortion after being dumped by swindler Cameron Fraser. And her congenital heart problem required a valve-replacement operation after the birth of the twins, **Lily and Freddie**. It seems to have maintained her get-up-and-go. During the summer months, she was up with the lark and out working on the memorial garden in a surprising alliance with **Lynda Snell**.

LILY AND FREDDIE PARGETTER

Lower Loxley Hall • Born 12.12.99
(Theodore and Madelaine Wakelin)

When **Elizabeth** was pregnant with twins, the family feared for her life, as she was suffering the effects of a congenital heart condition. But Lily and Freddie were born – in that order – safely if a little early – by caesarean section. **Hayley Tucker**, once their full-time nanny, fits the school run to and from Loxley Barratt Primary around her work organising activity visits to **Lower Loxley** for parties of schoolchildren.

NIGEL PARGETTER

Lower Loxley Hall • Born 8.6.59
(Graham Seed)

Nigel has more fads than a Japanese fashion victim, but most of them have in some way added to the **Lower Loxley** visitor experience. Recent crazes included raising vines to make Lower Loxley wine, restoring a ha-ha and building a memorial to his eccentric great-uncle Rupert (from whom Nigel perhaps inherited his idiosyncratic charm). Increasing concern for the future we're bequeathing to our children (in his case to **Lily and Freddie**) led to Nigel forsaking his car and developing the Hall as an environmentally friendly stately home, insulated with sheep's wool (no, really), heated by a woodchip boiler and offering 'green' weddings. It's just as well that Nigel has as his wife and co-manager the more pragmatic **Elizabeth**. His heart and her head combine to make Lower Loxley the success it is.

JAMIE PERKS

April Cottage • Born 20.7.95
(Ben Ratley)

Jamie lives with his mother **Kathy** and her partner **Kenton Archer**, although, being close (geographically and personally) to his father **Sid**, he regularly spends time at **The Bull**. Rather too much time for Kathy's liking during the prolonged residency of **Wayne Tucson**, the ageing rocker who was the first husband of Sid's current wife **Jolene**. Jamie was late home after Wayne started teaching him chords on the guitar. On a school night, too. Jamie's in the same year as **Daniel Hebden Lloyd**, although at different schools, which might explain why their friendship appeared to be drifting.

JOLENE PERKS

(née Rogers)
The Bull
(Buffy Davis)

The one-time Lily of Layton Cross, country music singer extraordinaire, went through a riot of emotions after former husband and fellow musician **Wayne Tucson** turned up at **The Bull**, homeless and sick with an alcohol problem. Jolene found herself at the centre of what the tabloids would call a 'tug-of-love' triangle. Wayne was trying to wheedle his way back into the life of daughter **Fallon Rogers**, herself a singer with the band Little White Lies. But was he also using his undoubted charms to pluck at Jolene's expansive heart strings? Her current husband, **Sid**, certainly thought so. Sid knows that he has a diamond in Jolene – still a fine figure of a woman, as **Joe Grundy** might put it. She's no mean businesswoman either. Since she replaced **Kathy** as landlady, Jolene has devoted her warm personality and generous 'assets' (tabloid-ese again) to building up trade and helping to fend off the effects of recession.

KATHY PERKS

(formerly Holland)
April Cottage • Born 30.1.53
(Hedli Niklaus)

The past year has been far better for Kathy than the one before. Not difficult considering the ordeal that she went through in 2008, giving evidence against a former colleague who had raped her. Gratitude to her partner **Kenton Archer** for his unwavering support at the time perhaps accounts for her tolerance towards his ongoing attempts to stay forever young – notably the tattoo and the nights out with the boys. But she was not happy about his apparent determination to turn **Jaxx Caff** into an upmarket bar, open all hours. With her demanding job at **Ambridge Golf Club**, she's worried that they'll never see each other. Also, her son **Jamie** is in need of a good male role model. She wasn't impressed when he went to **The Bull** to see his father **Sid**, and spent too much time with wayward **Wayne Tucson**, **Jolene**'s ex. If Kathy and Sid could agree on one thing, it was that Wayne's departure couldn't come soon enough.

SID PERKS

The Bull • Born 9.6.44
(Alan Devereux)

Sid has become a pillar of the community since he arrived in **Ambridge** as a young tearaway from Birmingham in 1963. He now runs **The Bull**, in which he has a 49 per cent share (with **Lilian Bellamy**), and is married to voluptuous **Jolene**. His first wife Polly died in 1982. Their daughter Lucy and grandson Matt live in New Zealand while **Jamie** – his son from his second marriage – lives in Ambridge with his mother **Kathy**. A keen cricketer for most of his life, Sid coaches at Loxley Barratt Primary and still takes an interest in the Ambridge team. While he would appreciate star batsman **Adam Macy**'s competitive captaincy, he has always found it distasteful that Adam is gay. Distaste is not strong enough for his feelings towards Jolene's former husband, **Wayne Tucson**, whose extended stay at The Bull nearly drove him to distraction.

HEATHER PRITCHARD

Prudhoe, Northumberland
(Joyce Gibbs)

Once a mother, always a mother, but the distance from **Borsetshire** to Northumberland means that **Ruth Archer** doesn't get as much hands-on mothering and grand-mothering as Heather would probably like. Widowed since 2002, Heather has a thriving social life and is quite comfortably off, as can be deduced from the number of cruises she takes. It's an interest she shares with relatively new-found friend **Jim Lloyd**, father of Ruth's brother-in-law **Alistair**. Does that make him father-in-law-in-law? And will their friendship flourish on one of Heather's visits to **Ambridge**, where Jim seems to be settling? We shall see…

FALLON ROGERS

The Bull • Born 19.6.85

(Joanna van Kampen)

Fallon's musical career hit a discordant period, for practical and personal reasons. The practical problem of substituting Finn in her band, Little White Lies, was compounded by the personal problem of dealing with her wayward Dad **Wayne Tucson,** who turned up in her life unexpectedly. Wayne knows about the music scene, having been on the road with his guitar for most of Fallon's life. Indeed, he abandoned her and her mother **Jolene** when Fallon was a toddler. No wonder she was, initially at least, bitterly resistant to his attempts to make it up to her after he stumbled back into her life and she brought him home to **The Bull**. Fallon is popular with young and old in **Ambridge**, as the promoter of music nights 'Upstairs@The Bull' and musical director of village shows. But after Wayne's whirl of emotions brought disharmony to a pub that has been her home and main workplace, she could be forgiven for hitting the road herself.

RONNIE

Farriers make a good living and are often popular with the ladies. We're not sure whether it was this or an interest in horse anatomy and metalworking which drew **Christopher Carter** to the profession. But in 2004 he managed to persuade Ronnie to take him onto the farrier's apprenticeship scheme. Ronnie's faith was justified in 2008 when Chris passed successfully – with only a few wobbles along the way.

GRAHAM RYDER

Borchester
(Malcolm McKee)

As a land agent working for the **Borchester** firm of Rodway and Watson, Graham used to supervise the management of the **Estate**'s 'in-hand' farmland. He was less than gruntled when **Matt Crawford** passed that role to **Debbie Aldridge** in 2006, leaving Graham with little more than collecting the quarterly rent from **Bridge Farm** – and even that task went when **Pat** and **Tony Archer** bought their freehold. Graham can't quite understand why he is so unpopular in **Ambridge**. He sees himself as courteous and conscientious but others interpret that as oily and nit-picking. Invoking the health and safety laws in a way that nearly closed down the village pantomime did little to boost his rankings in the local popularity stakes.

ANNABELLE SCHRIVENER

Felpersham
(Julia Hills)

Annabelle knows how to flatter a man. It helps that this senior partner in a law firm specialising in property has beauty as well as brains. Having flirtatiously played **Matt Crawford** along in a relationship that was strictly business from her point of view, she saw which way the wind was blowing once the Serious Fraud Office began investigating his dealings. Her manoeuvrings behind the scenes saw Matt replaced as chairman of **Borchester Land** by **Brian Aldridge**. Brian was easy enough to persuade once she fluttered her eyelashes and flattered his ego. In her spare time, Annabelle likes to run, sometimes with fellow lawyer **Usha Franks**, with whom she developed a competitive friendship on the build-up to the **Felpersham** Marathon.

SILENT CHARACTERS

One of the delights of **Ambridge** is that coterie of characters whom the listener knows well and can picture clearly but who are never actually heard to speak. A large but obviously rather quiet band, they include the ageing Mrs Potter and Mr Pullen at Manorfield Close; **Lower Loxley**'s gardener Edgar Titcombe and housekeeper Eileen Titcombe and resident falconer Jessica; **Eddie Grundy**'s friends Baggy and Fat Paul; **Home Farm** workers Andy and Jeff; **William Grundy**'s deputy Pete; exotic Anja at **Ambridge Organics**; no-nonsense Naomi, Polish waitress Ottie and burger flipper Frank at **Jaxx Caff**; bell-ringer **Neville Booth** and his unpopular nephew **Nathan**; **Ambridge Golf Club**'s director of golf Leigh Barham; the very fit **Sabrina Thwaite** and her husband **Richard**; the Button family; parish council chair **Derek Fletcher**; many of the **Horrobins**; and those latter-day femmes fatales Mandy Beesborough and **Freda Fry**.

LYNDA SNELL

Ambridge Hall • Born 29.5.47
(Carole Boyd)

Lynda is looking forward to being an inspiration to the new baby delivered by Coriander, husband **Robert**'s daughter. But how will she find the time? Bustling with energy as ever, she was getting up at the crack of dawn in summer to work on the memorial garden with fellow insomniac **Elizabeth Pargetter**. Since Elizabeth persuaded sculptor Anthony Gormley to attend the village fete, Linda's admiration for her has known no bounds. The arts are one of Lynda's great passions. At Christmas she has brought her talents as a theatre director to the village panto. Rampant hay fever every summer is no barrier to her environmental activism – most recently opposing **Adam Macy**'s plans to extend his poly-tunnels. Senior Receptionist at **Grey Gables**, Lynda also takes in B&B guests at **Ambridge Hall**, where she keeps pet llamas in the grounds. The fact that they are named Wolfgang, Constanza and Salieri probably tells you all you need to know…

ROBERT SNELL

Ambridge Hall • Born 5.4.43
(Graham Blockey)

Retrenching after the collapse of his software business in 1995, Robert made a decent living with a few small clients and agency work. But when a contract was terminated in 2006 he started to despair of finding another job in the IT industry. To his – and most of his neighbours' – surprise, he found a late-late second career as **Ambridge**'s genial odd-job man. And in 2007 he became chief cook and guest-greeter when he and **Lynda** started to take in B&B guests. Genuinely in love with Lynda (he'd have to be), Robert has two daughters from his first marriage. The younger Coriander ('Cas') has just given birth. Let's hope that Robert is better at holding on to babies than he is to descending cricket balls.

ST STEPHEN'S CHURCH

Established 1281

The dust is settling again on **Ambridge**'s ancient parish church. Long-serving churchwardens **Shula Hebden Lloyd** and **Bert Fry** were replaced by **Christine Barford** and **Neil Carter**, who is also captain of the bell-ringers. Bert's replacement was routine, but Shula left under a cloud over the controversial marriage of vicar **Alan** and **Usha Franks**. Organist **Phil Archer** has seen many controversies come and go over the years – the installation of a lavatory, the appointment of a woman vicar, the proposed scrapping of the pews... He just kept his head down and his hands on the keyboard.

THE STABLES

Located just outside the centre of **Ambridge**, The Stables is the home and business of **Shula Hebden Lloyd**, who bought it in 2001 from her aunt **Christine Barford**. As well as stables offering the usual range of full, half or DIY livery, there's also a riding school complete with indoor arena. Shula's husband **Alistair Lloyd** has his veterinary surgery on site.

CAROLINE STERLING

(née Bone, formerly Pemberton)
Grange Farm • Born 3.4.55
(Sara Coward)

An aristocratic bloom in the nettle patch that is **Ambridge**, Caroline found success in work – managing **Grey Gables** hotel – while suffering serial failure in love. She once had an affair with **Brian Aldridge**, although that hardly makes her unique among **Borsetshire** women, and her (eventual) first husband Guy Pemberton tragically died after only six months of marriage. But latter years have brought greater happiness, with marriage in 2006 to fellow hunting enthusiast **Oliver Sterling** and their purchase of Grey Gables from former owner **Jack Woolley**. Oliver's recent retirement from **Grange Farm** will allow them to spend more time together, concentrating on managing Grey Gables through the recession.

OLIVER STERLING

Grange Farm
(Michael Cochrane)

When Oliver arrived in **Ambridge**, after a divorce and the sale of his large farm in North **Borsetshire**, he was set for a gentle semi-retirement at **Grange Farm**, with a little hobby farming on 50 acres there. But, as joint master of the South Borsetshire Hunt, he met and fell in love with **Caroline**. They were married in 2006 and along the way became joint owners of **Grey Gables** hotel. Resented by **Eddie** for taking over the farm that the Grundys lost, 'Sterling', as he calls him, has nonetheless lived up to his name by offering sterling support to young **Ed Grundy** when he needed it most. First he trusted him to run the small herd of Guernseys which supply **Mike Tucker**'s milk round and milk for the unpasteurised cheese sold in **Ambridge Organics**. Then he leased Ed the farm tenancy and sold him the herd on very reasonable terms so that Oliver could at last retire and spend more time with Caroline at Grey Gables.

MABEL THOMPSON

Bradford
(Mona Hammond)

The mother of **Alan Franks**'s deceased first wife, Catherine, Mabel was originally from Jamaica but is a long-term resident of Bradford. She's a woman of strong views and her visits to **Ambridge** can often be lively, to say the least. Alan's engagement and subsequent marriage to the Hindu **Usha** (née Gupta) was simply too heretical for this evangelical Christian. Not only did it drive a wedge between Mabel and Alan, but it soured her relationship with granddaughter **Amy**, too. Still, Mabel is a warm-hearted woman and she has nothing against Usha personally – unlike **Shula** with whom she discussed spiritual dilemmas when they met on a bench in the churchyard a few months after the wedding. Mabel evidently sees it as her duty to support Alan and, if that means accepting Usha as the vicar's wife, then so be it.

SABRINA AND RICHARD THWAITE

Grange Spinney

Well-heeled occupants of one of the most expensive developments in **Ambridge**. Richard commutes to work but finds time to turn out for the Ambridge cricket team. Indeed, **Adam Macy** seemed keen to encourage him, as Richard has the right win-at-all costs mentality. As for the svelte Sabrina, she's a super-fit 'yummy mummy', whose appearances at village events from pancake races to pub quizzes prove her to be fiercely competitive. She terrifies the life out of **Robert Snell**.

ABIGAIL (ABBIE) TUCKER

Willow Farm • Born 7.3.08

Hayley and **Roy Tucker**'s joy at the prospect of at last having their own child together turned to deep anxiety when Hayley went into labour ten weeks early. But after an extensive period in an incubator and on oxygen, little Abbie developed fully and they were able to bring her home to **Willow Farm**, a much-awaited little sister for **Phoebe Aldridge**. Abbie seems to have accepted granddad **Mike**'s new wife **Vicky** quicker than most of the females in **Ambridge**.

BRENDA TUCKER

1, The Green • Born 21.1.81
(Amy Shindler)

Brenda found it harder than anyone to accept the ebullient **Vicky** into the Tucker clan. She thinks her father **Mike** has made a terrible mistake in marrying a woman who is busy transforming her old home with items of dubious taste while insensitively ruining the garden. In Brenda's eyes, Vicky is everything that her understated mother was not, although she insists that her opposition to the marriage has nothing to do with the late Betty Tucker. At least Brenda's own love life is on the up after a painful split from **Tom**, who is now her fiancé. If only her working life was running as smoothly. A 2.1 in marketing from **Felpersham** University doesn't go far in today's graduate jobs market, despite the practical business experience she gained working for **Matt Crawford** before things turned nasty. She has had to content herself with helping out in the dairy and writing occasional press releases for **Pat Archer**.

HAYLEY TUCKER

(née Jordan)
Willow Farm • **Born 1.5.77**
(Lorraine Coady)

Like most young mothers, this bubbly and attractive Brummie is busy trying to balance the demands of work and childcare. It's altogether a new departure for Hayley. For years she was a full-time nanny, enabling other mothers to go out to work. She now runs activities for visiting school parties at **Lower Loxley** while being mother to **Phoebe** (husband **Roy**'s daughter by **Kate Aldridge**, now **Madikane**) and **Abbie** – the result of a long hoped-for pregnancy after extended fertility problems. After years of trying to get on the local property ladder, Hayley and Roy found their housing problems solved in another way: by funding the conversion of **Willow Farm** into two residences. She now has **Vicky Tucker** living next door and off work three days a week, which might make that childcare balancing act just a little easier.

MIKE TUCKER

Willow Cottage • Born 1.12.49
(Terry Molloy)

Mike deserves a bit of fun after the death of his first wife Betty, bankruptcy from his dairy farm, a nervous breakdown and losing his eye in a farming accident. So who would begrudge him his evident happiness with his exhausting new bride **Vicky**? Well, his daughter **Brenda** doesn't think it will last, and a substantial part of the female population of **Ambridge** is sceptical – especially Betty's close friends. For now, however, he's enjoying being Vicky's 'Mr Bubbles', much to the irritation of his son **Roy**, who thinks this term of endearment makes Mike sound like her poodle. When he can drag himself away from Vicky's seductive charms, Mike's enthusiastically backing **Ed Grundy**'s plans to expand the dairy herd at **Grange Farm** that supplies his milk round.

ROY TUCKER

Willow Farm • Born 2.2.78
(Ian Pepperell)

Roy is an efficient and popular manager at **Grey Gables**. But the guests could hardly imagine his colourful past. Once part of the group of racist thugs who terrorised **Usha Franks**, Roy soon came to his senses and buckled down to business studies at **Felpersham** University. But while there he had a daughter, **Phoebe Aldridge**, with **Kate Madikane** and fought for his right to raise the child. He later married **Hayley**, and they've since had a daughter of their own. **Abbie** arrived in 2008. After Roy's sister **Brenda** withdrew her objections, they took up **Mike**'s solution to the challenge of housing the four of them, by converting **Willow Farm** into two dwellings. Although he has her living next door, Roy has adapted better than Brenda to having **Vicky Tucker** as his new stepmother. Vivacious Vicky would not have been his first choice as a bride for his old man, but he accepts that she's made Mike happy and put a spring in his step.

VICKY TUCKER

(née Hudson)
Willow Cottage
(Rachel Atkins)

Vicky divides opinion in **Ambridge**. Most men think she's a bit of all right and that good old **Mike**'s done well for himself (nudge, nudge, wink, wink). Well, he was a slightly paunchy widower of 59 when she swept him off his feet, and she's young enough and up-front enough to have flung off her clothes when she discovered a nudist beach on their honeymoon. The same body was crammed into a wedding dress that left nothing to the imagination. Looked like 'an explosion in a meringue factory', according to Mike's daughter **Brenda**, leader of a Greek chorus of female disapproval. Brenda feels that Vicky's not right for her dad. **Susan Carter** and **Clarrie Grundy** feel that… well, she's just not Betty (Mike's late wife). Having lived alone in **Borchester**, Vicky's trying a bit too hard to fit in to a village community. But at least **Lynda Snell** did her best to make her feel welcome.

WAYNE TUCSON

(Sion Probert)

When Fallon's Dad, ex small-time rock and country singer, **Wayne**, arrived drunk and sleeping rough in **Ambridge**, both **Fallon** and Mum **Jolene** knew they would be in for a difficult ride. And so it proved as, much to **Sid**'s horror, Wayne embedded himself at **The Bull**. Determined to bond once more with his only daughter, Wayne also made himself popular wth the darts team and with **Freda Fry** in the restaurant. As mother and daughter became embroiled once again in Wayne's life and concerned for his well being, Sid found it more and more difficult to get rid of him.

ANNETTE TURNER

Over the Village Shop • Born September 1990
(Anne-Marie Piazza)

Annette is the younger daughter of Greg, the gamekeeper who committed suicide – not a good legacy to hand on to your children. She felt in the way at the French homes of sister Sonja and their mother, who has a new boyfriend. So she was looking for love when she arrived in **Ambridge**. **Helen Archer**, Greg's former girlfriend, found room for her in her flat and offered motherly advice that has been ignored as often as her nourishing meals have been left in the oven. After Helen's brother **Tom** honourably deflected her advances, Annette enjoyed a brief fling with **Jazzer** before he dumped her. Clinginess is not a quality that appeals to this particular Jock-the-lad. Nor is he alone in that among the eligible singletons in Ambridge and district. At least Annette proved herself a promising saleswoman, having helped Jazzer shift his strawberries, Helen sell ice creams and **Susan Carter** sell almost anything in the **Village Shop**.

UNDERWOODS

Well Street, Borchester

Underwoods department store –
It's the store with so much more!

Kitchen, bathroom, under stairs,
You'll find the things that you need there.
We have clothes for all of you –
Ladies, gents and children too
And the things to feed them all
In our well-stocked fine food hall.
Looking for a present, fellers?
Try our helpful perfume sellers!

Underwoods department store –
It's the store with so much more.

Advertising jingle (rejected)

THE VILLAGE SHOP

The shop has been under threat for years. **Ambridge** folk are like anybody else: they do their main shop at the supermarket and pop in for a DVD, a bottle of wine, carton of milk or, in **Lilian**'s case, 60 of 'the usual'. Gossip is supplied, free of charge, by manager and postmistress **Susan Carter**. It was Susan and her husband **Neil** who persuaded **Peggy Woolley** (on husband **Jack**'s behalf) to refurbish and let out the flat upstairs to generate some much-needed extra income. Village shops have become an endangered species and Ambridge was only reprieved during the Government's round of post office closures when the axe fell on neighbouring Penny Hassett. Things may need to change to get the shop through the recession.

WILLOW FARM

Just when the house at Willow Farm was settling down again after extensive building work to split the property between junior and senior Tuckers, in breezed **Mike**'s new bride **Vicky** with her own ideas about interior décor on the Willow Cottage side of the divide. Mike really should have kept his sunglasses on when, soon after the couple's return from honeymoon, he found his kitchen redecorated to Vicky's requirements to match their new, over-sized breakfast set. For Mike's daughter **Brenda**, the décor was confirmation of Vicky's execrable taste. Her bother **Roy** lives in the adjoining half of the former farm house with wife **Hayley** and children **Phoebe** and **Abbie**. Nearby are eight acres owned by **Neil Carter** (the rest of the farm was sold long ago). As well as his own home, Neil's land houses his outdoor breeding herd of pigs and an organic free-range egg enterprise, run jointly with Hayley.

HAZEL WOOLLEY

California, Camden Town… who knows?
Born 15.2.56

(Annette Badland)

J ack Woolley adopted the daughter of his
second wife Valerie in 1968. Hazel claims to
work in the film business, but no one seems
to know exactly what sort of films. She made
one of her mercifully rare visits to **Ambridge**
in summer 2005 and only left having failed to
persuade Jack to sign **Grey Gables** over to her.
Peggy loves her dearly, of course…

JACK WOOLLEY

The Lodge, Grey Gables • Born 19.7.19
(Arnold Peters)

Having lost his faculties to the devastation caused by dementia, was Jack about to lose what was left of his fortune? Probably not. And he wouldn't know if he did. Like much else, the Woolleys' eroding bank balance was another problem for his battling (third) wife **Peggy** to sort out. As Jack's decline continues mercilessly, it's difficult to believe that he was once a shrewd businessman who bestrode the narrow world of **Ambridge** like a Brummie colossus. One by one, he was forced to sell his enterprises, including **Grey Gables** hotel, his shares in the ***Borchester*** *Echo* newspaper and **Jaxx Caff**. The bulk of Jack's care falls to Peggy. But for how much longer remains to be seen. The strain was telling on her and she's lost patience with an agency that sends a different carer every day.

PEGGY WOOLLEY

(née Perkins, formerly Archer)
The Lodge, Grey Gables • Born 13.11.24
(June Spencer)

Peggy has the resilience of an East Ender who lived through the Blitz. That stoicism has stood her in good stead as, despite suffering a stroke herself, she struggles to cope with the Alzheimer's visited on her second husband **Jack**. Her first husband was also called Jack. He was **Phil Archer**'s elder brother and an alcoholic – an occupational hazard for a publican. Mind you, it was Peggy who really ran **The Bull**. At least with Jack mark two she has support on hand from her children **Jennifer Aldridge**, **Lilian Bellamy** and **Tony Archer**, when she'll let them help. And son-in-law **Brian** has provided his financial adviser to cast a helpful eye over the recession-ravaged Woolley coffers. Tony wasn't happy about that. But even he must have been cheered to hear that there's more than enough to give Peggy financial security and still leave a decent legacy to her offspring.